My Kafka Century

by Arielle Greenberg

ACTION BOOKS

Tuscaloosa, Alabama

2005

Action Books
Joyelle McSweeney and Johannes Göransson, Editors
Jesper Göransson, Art Director
Kristina Sigler, Assistant Editor

Action Books gratefully acknowledges the instrumental support of the Office of
the Provost, College of Arts and Sciences, and Department of English at the
University of Alabama.

Action Books
University of Alabama, Dept of English
103 Morgan Hall, Box 870244
Tuscaloosa, AL 35487-0244

Learn more about us at www.actionbooks.org.

for my family,
the one from which I came
& the one I've been blessed to make

& for Rachel Zucker, another kind of family

CONTENTS

We are digging the pit of Babel.
—Franz Kafka

Kafka: take my hand so tightly
that I think you are taking it with you.
—Michael Burkard, "Kakfa Tom"

Who figures an immigrant's going to have a pony?
Who leaves a country packed with ponies for a non-
pony country? —*Seinfeld*

Ewe, or The One Who Brings Water

To begin: an impropriety:
to you: I send this missive of false
starts, half asleep, half in jest,
wholly imperfect I took the child from you
& X'd that aquarium court
yard with both our fear-sets flickering,
me and your algebraic boy,
our filaments inside an ancient jellyfish.
I am as needy as.
I cannot take another demon, fatigue, or.
I've enough, you wrote, your third
brain quivering in the glow
of the sad, soft world.

And what of the weather that would not behave?
Be stricter. Tell me again
it will not rain until we are empty as litter bins.
Give me another small letter I can keep
while the wolves come at me
We have headaches. You have nothing to teach us. It may rain
though still they dot my i's and bring
themselves closer to the fire.

So here I go, and you with your hands full of rice
and misplaced furniture: husband to *me*.
Attach *me*: thread of light I have: I do not have it.

Me and Peter Lorre Down by the Schoolyard

Me and my sidekick, we're both pederasts. Like you.
We're both in love with the girls, non-Jews.
Ja, ja, we dress in our mother's nightgown,
we hang all the way around, Hungarians in ruin.
Know us, our terrible noses, our clown makeup:
we have no papers. We crawled out of the rat-hole.
Like you, we wear our difference about our necks, blind as a fox stole,
its glass teeth, its yellowed eye. The little girls, they cry. Like I.
Please, policeman, heed our crime: ink the territory
like a six-sided star around where we broke the kid from her line.
They keep a record of each beggar, the names in a ledger,
and later you'll know the clove of our hoof. So clever.
Kindermurder—it sounds sweet as a game and we want food.
We've got a toy ferris wheel full of knives, we smear
our mouths into sugary smiles, then brandy, then into gash.
A tubercular rag, you've caught our rash, the balloon-man
making *nein*, one girl stuck in the telephone wires.
Lifting higher. We take them from their candy,
we take their names. Like you, they are never the same.

Please Be Good

Something big and ugly with a long thin tail, something white with mottled fur, something barrel-bodied. Something went shuffling fatly into the brush at the side of the road tonight. And then there was a silver field mouse being horrible and small on the driveway. Then a waterbug with its bristle of silky, tickling arms by the fridge. A secret let out. A scream. I am slightly drunk, slightly more or less like a girl: is this a door? A keyhole? A handle? A pervert? When I lean over my blood is in my ears. I sleep with my fear in there, vertigo, also blood again. I lean over as an experiment—sudden flush of pass-out ocean? Bug? Rodent? Yes, pervert. Yes, with a tail. Cockroaches actually inside my canals. Dreams actually swarming with vermin trying to come in all the window screens. I have come out of the walls. The rat is more or less a migraine. I am all suited up in roadkill: stole, collar, purse. I keep an insect here. These *are* my cleanest sheets.

Private, I

Mystery date, I felt up your history.
All along that corridor my arm went
like the zen inside a dead black cocktail glove.
I could just make out your victim-nubs,
just distinguish the traumas bumping around that canal of love.

Detectives, my eyes are damp as tunnels.
Below each one is a shiny punch patch
that stars out the ex of time, so private.
I cast a long skin shadow
and darken every corner with what's mine:
my blowing draperies, and my single eye-piece,
and my draped milk-white pearls
which I have pulled out on their silk strand
from the blood-hole, one by one, sobbing on the string,
and ring around the tubing of my dove-white neck.

Ocularium

I want back the arrows
I had as a to-sleep child,
bluelight, I want.
I solved something I could see—
a jagged acrostic,
each square a baby clipped
from the art of the eye.
There are others.
My vision bifurcated then
as low, and lo, I lost
an arrow in that thick field
lined with exclamations.
Age, a sum, a thing,
zipped down to its pocket,
jointed for two hands to meet
and pretend to be speaking beaks.
I removed my hands to shut
the lids. I closed my sight-shop,
and got zapped, or hoped,
a frieze off a cornea that blinked.

The Dybbuk

Come closer if you want to hear the dead boiling inside my poppy-hot mouth.
I smell like the grease of my kerchief. I tell you the throaty sense is a demon.
I tell you the demon is a boy I cannot silence.
You'll listen—he's a scholar. He knows every law by heart.

Gilgul (Rolling)

Some squat truth shoots out and bullocks,
I'm in to learn my lesson, I'm rolling with the afterbirth,
infantilized, poisoned into clasping yet close another soul,
rabid doll-parts, rabid skull.

Umbilically I thrust and churn—
it's only natural—I've lived again.

One lifetime of these will be my finish up.
One day G-d and I will double-date,
and I will get to know His middle dash up close.

Ibbur (Impregnated)

Say the man (!) has done it all right: his temple a birthmark, his studies a migraine,
his central story outlined in fine black ink, his hairy arms lashed
tight as whips and three times a day he sways closer to the promise of manna.
This is one of only eleven decents we've got going at any given time.
He'll (!) have to go around again, to guide the weaker life he's riding
to wisdom, to complete his soup of deeds or studies,
to make the body, his righteous poppet, do his dirty work.

Usually the living will grow thin within their bodies out of respect,
scoot over, and make room for the wise one who needs their forefinger of flesh
to point the way. Only the corporeal can make a mitzvah,
but like a cat or cow, mere humans grow fat with smarts.
The man (!) will come inside, be the moving fetus or heartstring,
until G-d has his fill of the goodness he (!) glows.

Dybbuk (Clinger)

Women are like rubies—they have black eyes.
They are pets. They are prone to evil-doings.
I am a bird, once. I am a beak or shrew.
This is my story.

A wise man decided he loved me but was poor—
isn't that how it goes? I don't know.
I spend most of my time in the oven.
Anyway, my papa picked out a moneybags
and that killed the one who wanted me
for dusting his red-bound set of holy books.
It didn't much matter, but now here is the golden husband
standing before me, holding a magpie ring and luxe veil.
It hardly seemed fair—one dead, one dumb as a nail
and twice as sveltely brutal. So I swallowed down
a spirit and called it a man.
They called it a man. No one could catch it.

Here's the trick:
1. Speak sotto voce, at the bottom of your well.
2. Pull and rip your curling hair.
3. Rave, and rave, and say great things, and be brave, and fling around chairs.
It's facile but effective.

I became medium, a rare girl.
The village, Pinsk or Minsk, wanted to know
what demon flourished in my slim freight,
what viper had wrested the woman from my soul.

It was so liberating. I began to make demands.
I made predictions—widows, miscarriages, business plans—
and became a crude Hosea until the rebbe showed up
with a mad bag of prayers to dissever me from my plot.
We shook down the house together—he manacled me,
but I hung on: I made the devil hormonal and it would not go.

I'd almost convinced myself, a swift tinge in my perineum:
maybe I *was* this special, a double creature, man and wife.
Certainly I'd never felt better in my life.
But finally I was weary. I tossed my ventriloquism
out the window where everyone said it would be chased down
by the cemetery gabriels and their justified weaponry.

I don't know. I am back to the oven.
I've married the dummkopf—I think he's in love.

Little Red Fox

Yeah, it'll chomp you. It does like meat.
It likes your leg. It looks so sweet. It looks like rain,
so cancel the invitations—if you throw a soiree,
the woodchuck will chomp you with its twisted
Indian name. So will the set of wolverine teeth,
unabated. So will the tribe—they're pretty pissed.
You thought you would escape the rats
but here you are, a groom
at the rat-wedding, tying down the wet horses.
It's now your job, not your colony.
You're the most eligible bachelor the new world has seen.
Such creatures, such fucked-up land.
Every bride's a hailstorm, every mammal
with a back jaw that unlocks runs
through woods. Did you know the sign of
carnivore, how it backs its arrow in the stars?
The rats are lovely tonight, moonless.
Dark and deep. But you look a bit owlish to me.
The voice of the branches with their death
coming out—that will chomp you.
That sounds like several maids of honor at once,
all sewn together in their matching gowns,
their long, thin tails, their Indian names, their prey.

Shirley Temple, Black

Human reason is a shutter that raps,
all dusty, in the countryhouse of the brain.
Go through the window and you become an animal,
and are so happy to lie in your little round bed, stuffed with cedar.

I mean that madness is a ship to back where our thumbs did not oppose.
I mean that this is where we relax back into our cracker shapes:
giraffe, platypus, wolverine, ape.
I want once again to be sold in a little box, a cardboard cage, a zoo.

I once got a photograph of Shirley Temple as a girl
at Christmastime meant to be sent to fans—she looked a little spooked,
and behind her head someone had written the greeting
in a hand that was supposed to be a kid's
but looked more like a psychopath's.
And I knew then that she was ambassador to cannibals,
the entertainment director on my losingest cruise,
the shutters of my eyes banging on their ruffled hinges.
I think I am most at home inside the ear of a dog,
sweet portal to lunacy, where no day is Jesus, and a kickboard
keeps me from bursting into yet another child star.

Pastoral

"Because the Jew and Nature, those are two separate things."
—Paul Celan, "Conversation in the Mountains"

This old schlepper, he was hungry. He was always hungry, and he was always broke, and he was stupid as a rock, and everywhere he went he was followed by his only friend, a dirty, scrawny goat. Yes, there are beautiful animals in the world, but this one was no looker, let me tell you. This was a disgusting, revolting old goat, with stink-grass in its teeth, and a long beard that had drool stuck in it, and crooked horns and yellow curling hair around its hooves from where it had stepped in its own pish. And the old man and the goat, for years they were like brothers, laughing, singing, but the man was hungry, he was poor, he had no money. So one day he said *Goat, what can I tell you? We've been friends a long time, but I'm hungry. It's time to be eaten.* And the goat said, *You're crazy in the head. Without me, you have nothing, not a little song to keep you going. No one else to put up with your stupid jokes all the time and your smell.* The man said, *My smell?* and the goat said, *Shut up and listen to me. We'll get you a good, fat chicken, and you won't need to eat me. We'll put some butter and salt, make it nice. You'll eat, you'll like.* And the man thought it sounded like not such a bad idea, so the two friends went off to find a chicken. Did they know how to find a chicken? No, of course not—they had pebbles for brains, believe me. But they thought, chickens are like birds. We'll listen, see if we can hear a song. And off they went through the forest to hear a chicken song. They went up and down hills, mud all over the place, it was raining, it was misery, let me tell you. Finally there was a song coming out of a tree. *Alright already*, said the goat. *I'm starving*, said the man. *Can I eat it raw? Hey, chicken! Come here!* And the song stopped and a songbird stepped out on a little branch and gave the man and the goat such a look. *What, are you calling me a chicken?* said the songbird. *I'm no chicken. I'm dying of no food*, said the man. *Where's the salt shaker?* The bird took a hop back on his branch and said, *You're the dumbest shmuck I ever saw. You don't tell an animal you're going to eat it before you eat it. Stupid in the head! Come on, both of you—we'll get a nice cow. I haven't had steak in weeks.* And so off they went, three jerks like you couldn't believe, nearly with cramps from the hunger. It was all bushes and thorns and god knows what, some kind of jungle almost, and it was night when the moon shone a light over an enormous milky-white rump. *Cow!* cried the man in such joy. *Go to hell,* said the woman, turning around, having just had a little bath in the river. The man looked at her with a crazy eye and said, *I have to eat you. I haven't had food in days. I wanted to eat my goat but he's my only companion. I wanted to eat this bird here but he's too smart for me. You're a big juicy girl—you got a fork and knife around here somewhere?* The girl said, *You can't eat me. I'm the same as you; I'm a person. Persons don't eat persons. It'd be like eating your mother.* And the man said, *I hope not—she was all dark meat.*

Scratch-Eye

The hour whips something at you from its dark clock-box—
it could be a buggy or a bird or a wisdom.
There's a road behind the house with no road behind it—
that's a neat trick. It brings beyond in closer.
The transparent coroner will have a fit
to see his rows of evened corpses
frou-froued up in lilies and asters in the middle of the road.
Welcome to the funeral for what you thought.
It's now falsely blushing for eternity.
The organ in the corner plays buggy music, wisdom music.
The ghost road is whipped by actual, streaming automobiles,
a devout soul peeking out each glass window
like a toy surprise caught inside.
It's a game you play with yourself on Saturday nights watching movies rewind—
it's called Scratch-Eye: rub once
and the house has burst into feathers,
rub again and the house has molted into flame,
a real live road teeming with the sad lashes of ghostly mourners.

Morning Breaks the Window

Unknowable covers the baby's head with lye
To keep it straight. To make it burn.
Unknowing wipes the sink with Crisco
Because the ironwork's so old.
The Un begins his wily day stripping
The skin from my lips. Polish, he says. New skin.
He is good with chores while I am shiftless and worn.
Together, we are a family.
I have played the Bad One like a mother. I am meant for it.

Morning breaks the window with its light.
The glass lies all around the house distressed.
Pain glints in the cups and saucers.
Mister X triumphant over his rancid lard.

And here I am, an alias to it all,
Waiting for the cue to pull me back to smarts.

Under the Damask

Lived a pretty disgruntled tiny house
—A behind the curtains life—still
As an ottoman ghost on poor
Feet—the way of the furniture.
Jesus didn't love it—the house
Felt. Wanted sex with velvet
(They all did—artists!) and cuddles
With cotton duck. Apolitical
Canvas. —Bad bad house—really pathetic
Loner—This was the song it sang
To itself—besides the one that went
Sweet sweet you rotten boxy junk.
Then it met a doll—poverty doll—
Living in a dust swirl—but unjaded!—
So fresh—the painted-on eyes of
A war bride. —Marry me, said the house.
Be the bustle in my kitchen.
Every cabinet a whitewashed burden
Awaiting your hor d'oeuvres.
I will stop making the attic wind.
Okey-doke, said the doll. I am
So gingham—Mindless with hunger.
I'll take even this pity garden on.
And it became a household inside
The household—just under the living
Room drapes—with the larger household
Only a dollhouse to the monster gods
Invented by children in their ever-
Larger more encompassing
Dollhouse—a universe of silks.

Some Dark Holler

I was waiting to be loved by kiddie-nappers
out there by the wellspring, in the willow brush,
the golden nap of pollen fuzz blurring me, and I was

in a lowly mood; I was worn
by the notion that once I'd worn a thousand uniforms
of twisted paper roses leaking pinkness and now was just

a pervert in brass, and squatting
like a beggar down where I'd been a lassie. My mouth
ran dry, my tongue ran like the wormy tongues

of the dark river, and in the bush
hid the blue-painted or yeller-painted
mysteriosos who had come for me, I hoped. I am only paranoid

in that I am always right about who is going to love
the bejesus right out of me. I waited
and waited for Nothing to come and claim me

but I was not even baggage for bastards
and Nothing came, Nothing did not come. I decided to rally.
I left my stocking to make it look like the skin of a crime scene.

In my stead, the leaves wrapped around another poor fool
with a middle initial buried deep in the soil,
like a bear-trap in the coming dark. And I was waiting
to wear the fur that wanted to foil me, to bellow,
the gleaming dusk a loving cup, a trophy for any victim
that gets sunk in its silvery throat.

Diptych

But the secret of art:
how we were elastic.

Once you & I were per-
fect. You were happy.

We each had a startle
with Marys. I pulled

a knife on your mouth
but we hid it, ate butter.

We made baby allies against
the chore-list, the choir.

Mostly you jumped up
while I was downed with bits of fur.

We delighted in hotel soap
bars. Sang the sugar song.

I'm still flushed. Still.
We had a neverending.

Had stories of forest lambs.
Had skulls & bad fairies for breakfast.

Now (a bad year, a war, a cheat,
an always) you are wasting.

Less of you per. No luncheon.
The snap of crème de menthe.

Hapless and sloppy second,
you were codeless, happy.

If I am your star-point
etching, look here. You *were*.

I have all of your silver lines
in my right hand wide open.

My Kafka Century

By which I mean I have come to this dark county a carpetbagger,
and left it in the body of a woman.

That I am a good friend to dogs;
that my father's thumping love for me churns me and makes me race the road.

That I spit under my tongue against childhood enemy;
that I wear a grudge like a brass star locket on a chain.

That my life is a kind of flag for Life in General;
that I am hateful and boastful and chosen enough to make such a claim.

That if this Life we speak about can be shared—
that it is full of black enamel typewriter keys and empty boats and things slither-
ing in corners

but also pirate's treasure, wrongfully acquired,
but occasionally spent in the service of some miniscule, temporary good

like shining in the earlobe of the one you love,
or tethering the cloth playhouse with its immeasurable weight.

Ok Hurricane

The folding table is totally a dirty sumofabitch.
You're so right. We all agree. And are alone,
because we're holding down the camp stakes with steak knives,
and only you are blowing through.
Blow through anywhere, we don't care: windmills, midnights,
catfights, clean new life by a lake we had put up gently, with string.
Make a devastate. We'll call you Dervish.

                  Dervish, meet Kali.
Kali, meet this one, the scavenger, "parentalized."
Meet the children she claims will run to greet her
as their goodly tents are swallowed up by her arms
and the militia of oh my god cowers under that damn sumofabitch wind.

I have the most rickety legs now, four of them.
But to call you Mom sounds weird in my mouth.

Analogies

Let's play Houston We Have a Problem in which Houston
is to space program as bubble is to astronaut as crown is to queen
as queen is a golden shilling in the shoe of every solider whose
heart she owns in a little daggered box.

Let's play Hunter
Bring Me the Heart of the Fairest Maiden in which
coffin is to promise as dwarf is to washing-day and drudgery
is a bramble of roses and thickets keep out villains from the bedroom.

Let's play Hiding from the Nazis in Our Secret Annex
in which attic is to linen closet as map is to romance as certain death
is to romance as gasoline is to showerhead.

The mutable child is more like us every day:
mute, mutated, mutant. As speech is to therapy.

Let's play Maryann and Mary Jane, Best Friends Forever
and Also Identical Twins, Run an Eternal Day Care
for Orphans and Autistic Babies Which Transcends Our Own Playing
So That Even When We Don't Think We're Playing We Are in which the babies
are to wheelbarrows as apple tree is to biting red ants as mint bush leaves
are to the secret names of boys as nightgowns are to cartwheels
as fireworks are to piggyback and you go first.

Let's play Veterinarian in which safety pin is to stitches
as Kleenex is to bandage for the amputated limb as you or I
are slightly more crippled for the better, from this game.

Center Field

I sure hope the aliens come and get me
from their dear place out in the corn.
We can play when they do: baseball, a game
with diamonds in it, and sing
a song with birds in it and nests in it,
and amidst all those twigs,
an icon among icons.
The aliens don't know these rules
as they creep along, wresting asunder
from its neighboring verbs,
little baby birds with stretched tongues
prying out the backs of their linear throats.
Come and get it, says the mama to her kin.
The mothership has made a yummy supper.
I live on this planet, I say again.
And do I hope to be the shortstop
when the aliens on their streamlined spindles,
all spooky in their foreign whirring accents,
lob a fast one over to center field?
I sure don't. I want to keep living here.
I want to be married to an earthling,
curled inside the homing device of an egg.

Joke

Two Jews on a park bench in late afternoon:
For this we moved to California?

Yes.
Yes.
It was for the air, for the getaway, for the bird
you can't bring home for supper as either entrée or houseguest
though you want a bit of each, flesh and company.
The bird that waits above your dark heads like a tiny horror.
It has its own bad history.

An eighth of evening falls on the path.
The bird doesn't sing.
It never has—you can't really call what it does *song*.
It's more like bleating.
A hand of God slicing through the dimensions to stop this latest sacrifice.

A Jew:
It's getting late. Let's grab the sparrow and get out of here.

The bird chokes in the hold but the park bench
pipes up anyway, *take me, too. I'd rather die*
at your table than be such a slave here in the park.

The Jew:
Forget it. You'd come schlepping back here in an instant
on your cloven hooves. A slave!
What do you know of enslavement?
You stumble *even in beauty. We're no serial killers.*
We're no victims. There is no such thing as a Jewish alcoholic. This is self-defense.

It is as rotten an excuse as any.
If we are not eaten, we become hungry, and then we eat.
In the meantime, why not have a little good conversation to help the food settle?
A little showtune for old times' sake?

The bench (desperately): *I don't care.*
I've only ever known flora. I want to die an interior death.

The other Jew:
A talking bench? For this I could have stayed in New York, God forbid.

The First American to Walk on the Moon Was Black

I.

and it was on your birthday.

Here's another:

she wore her hair in ropes
plated with white-gold mud, the god mud,
and it swung like holy as she rose.

And soon we will walk on the streetlights
to blindness, even the out ones,
even the crickets singing our anthem.

And she wore a feather and a ring and went higher.

Happy birthday.

II.

Do you remember Chuck Yeager,
because he walked away from Death,
his business partner, and lived to tell it?
He done it twice, Death in his charring suit
and the hero with his cheek-skins
flung back like a dog's.

But hey now. There's a space race
and the lead runner is spitting,
she's pushing back dust. This is a nation
of stars, nation Night, and it only lasts
half a world. At morning it will be
ocean and Death will belly up out of the waves,
a sopping, pinstriped monster.

But it was your birthday yesterday,
and it will be tomorrow, clearly,
again, your launch, mach dozen,
anniversary of heart tattoo,
and only you know how deep to reach for flame.

Saints

1) Knives of the Saints

I returned your book of poetry to the store.
I returned to the scene of the crime because once I'd had you
the words floated into a ribbon of type.
Because it was where we once slung violent hash.
I returned a favor.
I returned the box to its proper shelf
that made not sense to me smelling of lavender,
and it waited to be made into a miracle.
I came carrying my wings in my teeth.
I came to under the organza influence of your best slap.
I came out. I came around.
I came back like a cat, the kind from hell.
I came to believe I'd been returned.

2) Chives of the Saints

When the waiter said "you're *welc*ome"
she was waylaid, completely soup.
Dumplings healed her. Broth sustained.
Between the server and the servee passed
an Olympic torch of familyhood, a fruit crepe
of happiness. She was thankful for being welcomed
into his arms like a brown rice bowl.
She was thankful to be so single, so unbetrothed
to the service she gratefully received.
You are welcome, she thought of herself,
an utter dish festooned with gratuity.

3) Lives of the Saints

Most are quite ordinary.
They speak in English, the tongue of regular paperbacks.
They read for awhile, looking occasionally away.
They get hungry at the usual times slated for hunger.
They do not write the menu in script on a chalkboard held by a ceramic pig in a toque.
They simply make humble but delicious
grilled cheese sandwiches, pressing their handprints
into the flaming bread, branding it,
blending ascientifically four kinds of cheese, including a dry jack.
They prefer to drink along a tomato juice.
They like to later drag a bicycle down from its stern hook and squeeze the wheels.
They like to spend time in the garage, damply almost dying on purpose.
Then they go back inside the split-level ranch and eat potato chips,
casually licking the bottom-of-the-bag salt from their fingers.

Everything Natalie

I'm thinking of the girls I don't love and how I love them.

I'm thinking of how ants burrow in a cluster of anthood under my pillow, which is disgusting, but how clusterhood isn't, how it's like loving a bunch of women whose heads are together like posies, and I'm thinking how I drunkened those ants and soon they'll die and that is no act of love.

I'm thinking of Natalie, how once I would not have loved her. In fact, there were days and years when I didn't love her, wasn't open to that kind of love, but today I love her and all that is open, and how if everything is a gate that opens, everything could also be the name of a poem, and everything is how it feels to be in the back seat of a station wagon at a drive-in, and everything is fireflies, and somewhere else everything is lightning bugs.

I'm thinking of how people love a firefly but not an ant, and by people I mean me. But would I love a firefly under my pillow? I might, if it glowed. Glowing is a love action.

I often think of how lightning seems to be missing a letter, it's so sudden.

I'm thinking now of how often I use so sudden.

I'm thinking about minutes, to be honest.

I'm thinking about you a lot more often. To be honest, I just tried calling you again, but you weren't there. Had you been, I might have asked you to come up tonight to where I am, in all this rain, and put your head on this slippery pillow, and be my cluster, my Natalie.

I'm thinking of the sound of rain because it's raining. That's easy.

I'm thinking about the beauty of a cluster of heads. Beauty is an action of love. Love is a beauty action.

I'm thinking about gesture.

Now I'm thinking of the minutes that belong to Natalie.

I'm thinking of how we bunched up in this bed here one night, the sheets bunched up, how I put poison in the corners of the room, how I could call you but it's too rainy, how everything is the back seat of a love action, and how that's not a metaphor—it's a seat you remove the headrest from and pull down flat and love to watch a movie out the back in the air, its cluster of glowing night bugs.

At the Cinema Lecture

<The crazy woman walks in, speaks some low French, and makes all our fingers stink of something balsamic, vaginal, or close to the roots.> <We hold these fingers close to our noses and inhale because it's embarrassing and disruptive.> <We need to get beyond the body because it's all theory, theory, theory.> <Our hands are dead, but if we were really dead, we could remove them and the way they make us smell.> <It makes us feel crazy.> <We do and do not want to be graduate students of the enlightenment.> <We do and do not want to be toll booth workers, handling the stinking money of strangers.> <The crazy woman whispers to us because we are her neighbors.> <Our extremities, our lives, our livelihoods, are institutionalized.> <It is an extreme state.> <Ghosts, dragonflies, moonbeams, the beautiful and irreal—we have this in common with the lecturer.> <We have it in common with the crazy woman, inserting our most internal smells into her own foreign language.>

Home Décor

What I write about That Time will be beautiful,
except for when it's not beautiful.
Can you believe I am full of such rich ideas.
For a person who cannot spit, I am remarkably full of clear fluids.

Stupidly (with a stupidness wholly new) I imagine
a vast bruised sky and me in it,
dumb Tinkerbell made of cotton candy,
lucid dreaming towards a duck pond or soda fountain.
I sort of float. Meanwhile, nothing is laundered.

This is my method for tricking my body—
I murmur *be so fat and useless* and it softly complies.
Honestly, the beautiful lines are for gardens, another thing about which I'm stupid.

Collecting the birds I've collected does not make me good or elegant,
does not build anyone a plain brown nest.
I'm done buying books in which the home décor spreads out like butter.

Folding the Bed

Bedmaker. Spoonmaker. Carpenter. Crook.
You've left me with nothing. My braids tied in silk.

Last night I dreamed I was swallowed in emeralds.
Morning came and the bookie took all.

You were the loan shark.
You greased my pockets.

I've got nothing left but my face on a nickel.
I've got nothing but down and a wrung-necked goose.

Forgive me. I'm wrongly. My head's in the larder.
I need just a knife and a pinch of your sugar.

I need just a slug of the gin in your bathwater.
I need just a tub. Just a song. Just a lick.

Make whisky from kettle.
Eat it like smoke.

I've loved this man up right out of his shoes.
I've loved his name up so it's all gone to leaking.

I've taken a rib to neaten my corners.
John Murphy. John Henry.

John Riley. John Doe.
There's a bird in the milk so there's none now for coffee.

One body is naked. With two you get questions.
Three for a song from before I was born.

Four for the bed resting inside the wall.
Five for shotgun. Six for shack.

Seven for the woodstove
stocked only with embers.

The winter is a frigid bitch bride who's my sister who smacks me.
I'll make a new bench from the tongues of the liars.

Remember this house cause you'll come back tonight.
Bedmaker. Spoonmaker. Carpenter. Crook.

It's Wednesday &

late. I've come to limp again, willful
toward the place you light up, that safe
good cage. It's been more of the bad games
with books & traitors. With one fair limb,
I unspool, darn into you. Want to rob
you & leave gold in place of the silver hooks
for good, start again with just skin.
My everything takes the edge off an apple.

One wants only a golden pincushion
on a velvet ribbon around the wrist while marking
the place with chalk of trying to mark it.
It could be a calendar or jewel or a dress-
pattern of me. One (me) wants
the spare, subtle craft of your arching,
to be lost & found in it,
a bed-coat sewn full with geese
who are here now, squared with home. As we are,
heads tucked under our tracing paper wings.

Helen of Troy: even she was not so outrageous
on the days she finished at the factory
with the steam-makers & pursed her mouth full of pins
against the plain round clock. Even she,
& not one thing rings around my eye
nor sticks as close as you could,
who knows me (an odd girl) even
with all my ships undressed of their better sails.

Dug Out

I'm a whirring arena in the middle of neighborhood,
a tweaking
bird. What are you?
My head is a see-through stadium,
jagged in its innings
and too hard to swallow.
What bird name are you in this lingo?
What tree on which street? I'm a Green thing
[my name/color field] without wanting it I don't know when to feed. I'm
skin. A night-game
waving to all the people coming
home to their expectant boxes
and light-up dinners.
To their niceties. You are a bad
habit. I'm, well, tweaking
on the nation's favorite pastime,
panic in the commute, panic. And you.
And me, I'm the train, whining
scraping and broken,
on track through the last vacant hotel
in your heart.

Note to self:
Turn the light out when you leave.
Turn all lights out.
Let the grass grow while it sleeps,
and make a diamond.

Letters from Camp

Dear. It's like camp, our ivy union,
those buried dollars. It's like summer:
with each breeze, I get a box.
I'd better. It looks like I'm writing
you a letter. Love. Stop. Dear.
The artists are a brat. I slake
down a sandwich and run
for the mail. We sit around shop,
talk girl talk and all the girls agree—
in their slots, they'd prefer
mostly men, a bit of boy,
a pleading drunk. It's so hetero
around here. I am finding
new ways to touch the leather.
I prefer tape (can you hear
me?) and the newsprint
crushed inside, turning my skin
to type. You are my type
if only you'd grow back your hair.
Love. Stop. Dear. Here's
a postcard of my needs:
I want to see a wild animal
and tame it like a brute tongue.
I want to be fluent in the forest,
naked. I would like to release
the moths from their pulsing
quiver chest. Love. Stop.
P.S. I'm nothing like an arrow.
You would barely recognize me.
It's all the whites they change for us,

every Tuesday. Dear. Here's another request:
I would like you to send me the chain
made of lettered keys. We can spell
that word you mentioned. We can make it
quite an elegant fight. You'll be divine
if you send it priority. And a clock. Love.
Stop. Dear. I'd like a letter.
You sent a plastic fox to sit at my window;
a plastic lamb to by my bed. It made
us both laugh. I wear the ring
of watery compass so I won't get
lost again. But the woods, honey.
The what comes from trees.
They feel like poison willows.
I'm scared of the dark at night,
what it doesn't have lying in it,
its ominous rocks, so I walk back
in twos. I've made some friends.
Love. Stop. Dear. I am writing
home, saying save me from this whiskey
sour. My only sidecar should be you.

Valentine

About to board a plane back home,
if you are looking for what's beautiful,
it's *us*, beautiful. Stupid.

I've always known. Scorpio. If I let you go,
out of the pony-box like a pony,
would you not come back with a basket full of filigreed eggs,
marbled eggs, chocolates, excelsior? Would you not triumph?

I say the shape *chas,*
then the shape *chalilah.*
In my father's religion, these will keep the truth out of my next ideas:

Some people, unnamed, do die in a plane crash.
Some young couple, my age, your age,
riding in a car you or I might buy,
in the backseat of which is carefully strapped
a strapping child such as we might have,
driving an upstate New York road we have traveled,
came to be underneath the age and heft
of a blown-across tree, across five lanes,
and they, us, lost in the moment of it.
Found, the baby alive, the mother crawled back to it
but dead. And the father.

Chas. And *chalilah.*

The hand of god is dark and womanly.
We were pitched like two china figurines across Monument Valley.
You wore terrible sweaters your mother chose.
I came with my superior methods of screaming.
We both settled in a town known for ill will. There was a tornado.
In a fit of seriousness, I composed verse about health care.
You discovered me, the weak crystal in a dull rock,
and made it make the no sense it made in front of everyone.
The week your first slept in my bed all the trees went pink
and something in that town was a perfect grilled cheese sandwich with fries on the side.
This is our story.

Later, we write a story for a movie in which one person lives two lives,
flying her Cessna back and forth like a folly. We give it a clever name.
We do not finish it. We barely start. We are mostly interested
in what she eats in either home,
and not the murder mystery that lights the plot.

If it's raining tomorrow, do not fly home,
much as home is mine and I am in it and without you
the dog sleeps in the hall, both of us a little rattled.
If it's raining tomorrow, wait it out.
Because of that thing we did last June with rings and wreaths of lavender,
I will be here also when it clears.

When it clears, come lose yourself with me under cabbage roses.
Come lose yourself with me in a triangle,

an underwater room made of chiming ghosts.
It's stupid how beautiful. When mostly happy
& finally found, what else is there to do but write it down,
golden eggs, sugar eggs, hollow egg
with two lovers made of frosting lost in the sparkling world inside,
sublimely plotless, in love with it?

Cannibal Flotation Device

The boys and girls all love the mean mom.
She's not that mean; she just holds her hands back skinny,
looks through glasses and says, "That's not what I meant"
and they are all about her so smartness.

One brother is a shock. Two sisters, hair falling.
They do not read this magazine and they do not watch this movie.
They live underwater where the poppies do a wavy dance;
they live off of a narcotic joke, a sour street that's eh, okay.
They're cannibals. Their cannibal flotation device comes in useful.
So do their incisors. They take family vacations together with the dog tied up,
everyone working harder on pieces.

I go noticeably without. No one eats me up or loves me so.
The dreams are not sweet: they make aliens,
and although I leave a little rhyme or two tacked to a tree,
I have no friends in the cannibal clan station wagon
when we come home tra-la from pee-wee soccer practice.
Some might say lucky you, but who would they be talking to?
I have horseshoes for eardrums.
It makes me liquidy sad, like the sound of a piano.

Secret Lesbian Tee-Off *for K.H. in Pat & Mike*

This is the most hallowed technical college on the block, and
       she, gymnasium siren, my jetty, belongs to nada,
       not even her "widowed" rectangle of torso:
       Katharine Hepburn, all rocky little eyes and angles.
       Darling. She boxes. When her beau returns, clum-
       sy, nodding, assigning names and numbers, she
       bites a bit her girlish hand, gets distractible. Dash.
       Leave off. Who needs him? This is a school for
       eighteen holes of scandal, each the glint of a dare
       and we won't tell. Tee dance, it's technical, ivy-cov-
       ered, a wondrous exam that takes continual place in
       the locker room: Mixed doubles. Add an equation.
       Build an architect of nice shot, honey. Kate-oh, we
       are the hall of famers' pairs of pals. Some sports-
       caster calls *The Babe is on the green* and we're just shy
       of it, mowed over, so well groomed, in slacks, mind
       your language. Let's us go have a quick sandwich or
       something. Your hair, Katie, it's mussed. Oh, is it?
       You tight kit. You meatless choice. Change into
       something in the backseat of the jalopy. Let's us
       benign the athletic program with our faculty whites,
       sweet fallacy, our thickened thigh, you and I, let's.
       Kate, you're mine and you're mine.

Doll Farm

I would like to openly tell you what I saw
but 1) somewhere along the road I added two letters to my name,
and this makes me slightly unaccountable.
2) I am also known to propose dances that have only one or two movements in sum.
3) When playing Peter Pan I will insist on being Tiger Lily.
4) My night vision is poor even with corrective lenses.
All of these statements are true, but you can see I lack sincerity.

Let me instead build you a farm out of some foamcore—
I mean a doll-farm—and make chicken-dolls from acorns,
paint some stones I collected to look like sheep.
We can gather popcorn for the eggs our hens lay and branches of pine for the trees.

It is not the best I can do.
I'm sure if I tried I could produce a line or two about Nature,
or reveal some near-religious sudden starry idea that a million people have had before,
but as I said, I am a person who added, for rather shoddy reason,
two extra letters to what used to be an upstanding, austere-ish name.
So let's just open this little matchbox drawer and take out berries to be apples
for the horses made of corks.

Newly Engaged to Jason

Your child spilt the perfume, so stank of perfume,
and your older child wet and soiled himself, on purpose, again and again.

The purpose of your birthday is to remember that a mother made you.
The purpose is to buy a special perfume, and break it,
and sit in that shit all day long, hating what makes you gorgeous. You say,
Today I am a special creature who was made by nobody.
I stand at the edge of the water and sing the song I invent
until I am interrupted a hundred thousand gazillion times.
I give all my precious objects to the ones who will kill them.
Here, my love, sit here and break Mama's vessel head.
Just sit quietly and don't die. If you do, it will kind of be your problem.
Because I made these children, I can kill them.

No one says that. You have never said that.
You would never, ever say that.

I do not have any children yet, so I do not have a birthday.
Happy me. My day is a cycle, so full of myself am I.
My stomach is smooth as champagne, weirdly lost of its button.
I am No. 5 with the cap off—every stranger senses how newly I am engaged.

I saw a play about a mother killer for no special purpose—
just because I have no children and can see any play I like, late at night,
without screaming, except the screams of the children
kilt by their mother in the famous real tragedy of ideal lives.
I am too young to have children, and too, too old,
and yet I felt for the heroine in her flat-foot exhaustion.
Every object I keep on my bureau looks like its Greek translation:
silken, fossilized, barren as rock. Enraged before its time.

I am hosting a party for the Argonauts of my fiancé.
We will have escargot and cocktails with cassis,
and it will happen whenever I like, all day long,
with people moving freely in and out of the breakable rooms,
climbing on the highest shelves, acting like tattooed sailors.
And I can sit out the whole thing if I want to, a classical cycle
on the toilet of womanhood, with the bathroom door utterly closed.
You are you, and have to go now, or be intruded.
I can sit here with my roses, and my urine.

Heenayni

Here I am, your fondest lugnut,
a shifting kitty towards the star of you
floating across a constellation of tattoo,
the firmament. I am firmly. I am yours.
Heenayni, Here I Am. Here I am, God.
I love you. I swear I'm not hiding.
I don't know where that palm frond came from.
I'm all yours.
Your drifting sheep-herder. Your pile of wool.
I know, I know. I know what you're thinking.
I got a bit caught up in the fratricide.
But I felt like I was glowing barium I was so findable,
his blood an x-ray through my blood.
He bloodied my indignant before he fell,
but I held on to the squint.
I went South. I didn't forward the mail.
But I was just waiting for my next instruction.
I thought that last arson was my sign.
So I stayed in Arizona. I wasn't hiding.
I was listed. I was in Tempe.
I was washing dishes.
Maybe you couldn't find me for the suds:
it was all kind of squeaky for a while there.
But I've returned, your mistrial,
your yellow morning cake.
Heenayni. As you know, I was never gone.

Honey

I am three months out and six to go,
stuffing my plastic Superball body with the salt
& twang of crackers die-cut into the shapes of fish.
God forsakes me when I forsake him
but mostly he's much kinder, as is his duty:
I am radiant, people tell me, and have no hives,
except the swarm of gold bombs biting its way
into my sticky hollow. And I don't mean sex.
I am just a menagerie for bright orange creatures.
Even my dreams are godless (and full
of God): I dream I am guided
by an elderly couple in a dim farmhouse
to their morning radio and blackberry tea
and then given the combs which I snap
into my dry mouth where they fill and fill.
Never, upon awaking, have I been so empty
and wanted more a cracker. Never so
suffused with the weekly, with time
as another god passing through the many perfect
crypts and ambers I house beneath my skin.

One Hundred and Eighty

When I become a mother,
the hole in my heart will gasp a song of old world violins.
This, like all other stories, keeps me awake: a pack of lies,
a pack of wolves, animals who make
the machine of the future, the future
into which, like a transparent silvery tube,
I will make a child. The child will be made of glass.
I will be the glassmaker's daughter, blowing a wish
into the burning, spinning hive.

Here's another story. There's this forest.
One could cut infinite paths in its snow,
but for argument's sake let's say one hundred and eighty are possible.
Let's say life is like this, a horrid story
of the Black Forest, and so there are paths with roots
and rocks and wolves,
and only one path paved in true blood,
the blood of what is real.
If one is real, then this is the only path one can find.
No others present themselves.
The right have no choice but to be right.

I twist and twist and cannot find it.
Or I find it and the blood tastes sweeter than it should, familiar.
Or I wander forty years in this forest,
switching back on myself at every wrung-neck bird.
The story is quite old, familiar, and see-through new.
When I become a mother, no matter how many books I read,
I will feel unprepared. I will feel betrayed and lied to.

I will want to read more books.
The books will make me crazy. I will break a fresh path
and lead myself to bears, caves, ravens, birds of prey.
I will double back, wear down the paths I've been told to try.
There will be no chocolate eggs and no tiny golden figurines
hidden politely under cabbage leaves. But a real egg. A real tiny.

Wake up. You whom I've married, I know when I hold you
I am only holding a part of what is yours,
what I mime to own. Doesn't matter which part.
Sing that song full of violins again, sweet song, while I am still a woman,
no one's mother, and just the same cannot go to sleep.

Red Rover

1.   I do not see you over there,
       waving at me with your eight long hands,
       your loose kid gloves made of bone buttons and skin.

       How are you, friend, across the milky highway?
       This blood-moat, a fairy tale made of lost teeth?

       May I come calling on your castle someday soon,
       with its myriad needles, its pretty fancy thorns?

2.   I am hollow as a doll, placidly waiting for the sever or chant
       that will break me over to your side.

       Then I, too, will be mutant. Activated. Blinded.

       I can't wait.

       What I wouldn't give for one night in your fucked hospital
       with all its flapping, sick-green gowns.

       What I won't give to be *ripped straight through,*
       gone through the fire ring, through.

3.   You see me and how I don't see you.

       You hear me singing all my most hollow tunes with little animals in them,
       the pathetic ballads that go *what I wouldn't give for your sore and lousy zoo.*

       About how I, too, will be made of soft, peeled-away flesh, too many tentacles.

       If I might. If I can.

4. If I cross to you, through your many alien arms, crashing, lifting,
    will all my songs be sucked from me
    in your repair shop for ever-broken things?
    And will it feel right?
    Will I then be as perfectly permanently damaged, go horizontal
    where once my seams stood straight, go slack, go over?
    And will I love it like I think I know I will but don't?

    I cannot hear so you so you cannot tell me.
    The rushing roars between us.

5. Call me over, you bad blue fairy. Terror. Mother.
    Let me come over.
    Cut my happy strings, and make me a real girl.

Report

I did that thing you wanted me to do.
I whispered the report of it to you as we lay
        in the trench-night, feeling the letters form
        at the sharp edges of all our hairs.
        The bones in our wings bent and shaped.
It hurts to kiss that way, but that is how we kiss:
in the family way, in the dark
        voided body the moon left as its husk,
        both of us a million tired gems
        swelled and lonely as the sky,
        hung together in our couplehood.

I did what you demanded: *get it together*.
How it hurt, my semi-self, my _____ bigged up
        inside my evening claws and my stomach
        and it did not own me nor was owned by me.
The moon was a stranger to the task you asked of me,
is, but I held you blind in our sweet new ditch.
        I made the sound that all bats make
        with the ends of their throats to tell you
I'd done that thing and done it for you.

Stag Movie

I have never had the pleasure of being shown the film in which the hart,
somewhat melancholy and gilded (I mean his antlers touched
by fairies, I mean delight of/in the sadness of the hunter
who must be borne to kill his passage in the fullness of his
being), fleetly tears through the spindled forest of his Creator's
stolen diary, at night; I've never seen the script which, I've been told,
like a diary, has hearts peering through all the craft-paper pages,
and sprinkles of glued-on glitter, and dictionaries, and cut-out stencils,
and each page a master painting, a labor of true love on the part
of the hunter (who employed animals like actors because she was from
a country where they speak the language of shadowed trees, taught in
little one-room schoolhouses that perch on frozen lakes like ice-fishing huts year-round,
a black country, with black trees, black days, one swollen midnight sun a year);
but when the will o' the wisps glow in *that* night (inside the film that can't
be seen by me [the film in which a chase is shot abstractly through the specter
of the desperate wearing sadness of the deer who is hunter, hunted,
mounting terror with his pack] because it is so spooled and black and curling
in someone's attic language, spooky lair, or archive), they glow even hazed
but all the whiter, brighter, silver, in my city garden picnic, the dark moment
that I'm being told by strangers who will seduce me, try to impress me, kiss me
full as wine and almost miss my mouth under the thin arbor that has no fruit or ivy,
as I'm only being told about the diary of the storyboard of the foreign,
abstract movie of the secret mournful qualities of the adult, raging hart.

The Edwardians

Is it President Taft who gets me going, restless with permission, back up on my cycle? It is truly President Taft, and I am wild with him, and sore.

In my love affair with President Taft, I call him Howard, and he is sweet on me, and on all sugared things. This makes me sweet on him. He deals me fake money, wants more and more chocolate inside his stiff paper shirt-front, and to me he is a dreamboat, sitting at his dining table, refusing to leave, and me on the banana seat sex of my cycle.

I tell my dear friend, *Buy my car—I don't need it anymore.* Sexual feelings make me generous in the morning. *I'm going to live at the World's Fair, I tell her. With my mister, President Howard Taft. You have children—I have none. My life is stuffed with candy.* This city ends under a Ferris wheel, and my very favorite car is turquoise blue and baby pink and swings with the tufted breeze of the colorized ocean shore.

But my friend cannot buy my car, even though, she, too, is paid with the fake money—the blue and pale pink money of the times, the kind that makes the world go round. It is June; I am having an affair with a gallon container of strawberry and vanilla ice cream by not eating it myself; I'm in love with the one who does, and is President.

Purple Noon

for David Trinidad

Now and again, you step into a boat
knowing full well that only Death will sail on
with you: you and Death, pretending
to play at cards, having put the girl ashore.
In this way, you remain a mystery to the fishermen;
a mystery, and a waste. They mutter. You pull
the hotel sheets into the shape
of Someone Else's insomnia
while you sleep with your arms back,
mouthing His name into mirrors, into the sleeve
of His silky dressing gown. You *feel like Him,*
but sometimes your arms pull back.

Man you love, girl you put ashore, name
you forge nightly, in fits of too-rich dreams.
After the kill, a chicken salad sandwich.
And always behind you the dark-haired lady
detective pressing the taste of you from her mouth
into a neat Italian napkin. You make sure no self-portrait exists,
and imagine a drowning, nap as if drowned.

You are fluent, liquid, but in the end it's a phone call
which will lure Him from the sea on a tangled cord, your Jailer,
Lover, the girl screaming from the shore into the silencing sun,
and something about the cliché *in plain sight*
darkens and pulls into white,
like the halo on a fresh bruise.

Unspoken, Sunbeam

Let me break you from your fugue,
small fuzz, twin god.
Here's an invitation made from glue:
Come to be. I'll sing you.
Morning (you). You'll
and night our skin and stars.
I will share with only one half
other. Broken from me,
the soft shoe at the end of vaudeville.

*

I will carve you from
this bright red chart,
carry you from room to room
in a dangerous heat.
Bee who means everything,
who doesn't sleep. Wordless.

*

I will carve you; I am not your wife.
Twin who opens. —half a bean.

Not your widow.

*

Hey, harbinger.
You are enormous, with soft hairs,
with your wettened father
and mother behind the lightning.
You lasted the forty hours your mother lost
and I now steal.

*

My back is loose and empty.
My vitamin is taken twice.
I am waiting for you alone, like any egg,
sating the dog, acting I don't care
I do care and the secret swells and swells
all along these faint biographies.

I have a lot of passages,
but only one for the hour of you.

Kafka Bicentennial

∝   A Country Doctor

As they say, born old.
Winter brings its white rape,
its endless wormy prostrators, each sudden,
expected as a guest—
that's the belief, anyway.
We (who?) sing the Hallel, a grace after rape,
the tuneless of the hills dancing their demise,
and woe of fever.
Another chosen pervert—save you, save they—
hushly drops enchanted sodomy onto its favored child.
The horses, in their glittering rape bells,
stir like Russian moons.

∝   The Hunter Gracchus

Pirates have been known to paint a small coin or altar made from bone
or tusk for their principal mermaid, even now that the mermaids
are headachy and unreliable. And so: an altar
of native man, shivering in the grasp of his body.
This guards my body, a folksy shield, lines my endless raft,
turns an altar from under me where hell shifts in waves,
a rocky sea of eyes. All the centuries
I am watched by that hourglass of pirate art,
and my legs are green wood, and cannot be ignited, moldering in gold paint.
Call it a coffin, sit by me: do not call it a lifeboat. Marine is my sight,
bottomless as a middle. My body's a bed. It seeks sheets.
In the pirate's best dream, little floating token, a maiden throws seed
to the sharks and they pool around for blood.
I am veiled with ancient forestry, from whence the wolves,
their cry—the whole universe has turned its windows out,
become the night of fifteen hundred dry inns.

Vagabond

I could be that one-eyed girl,
rapiste (the one who is, and
artfully is talked about). I could
be a vagabond, gossipmonger,
named for a saint and in a ditch.
I could be a bag of bones.

Bone-keeper, whisper the wish
I've already filled for you
like a doctor's order. With each
pill you take I get smaller,
until I am just, a little saint,
pitiful as new construction in autumn.

In your country, there's a city,
and then all the rest is wind,
and all the good words
are girls. *Filleted. Window*
I can never remember which sex.

What Would You Do Without Houses?

Or what without Louise? All the students come late, picking the easiest poems they can find. What will you do post-library? Will you end each line on the up and up in your speech as if you were British? What will you do to practice for the farce? You have the lead role. You are the force. You play the "intelligent, attractive young man." When the lights go out you do not glow even though you are that white. You are nearly gold. Some of us are. Some of us do not own a house. Others do not even rent. Louise is the leader of the writers. The students all turn their pages at the same time like an orchestra. Louise is the conductor. Louise is a train. What would you without her? You would complain. You could seek revenge but you know down deep it is not your own fault but you do keep going for the scissors. The younger you are, the lighter your hair, in some cases. In other cases, darker. In Louise's case, her hair never had a color. And she doesn't own a house. They put on lawn chemicals around her. You did. So yes, you are greener. You complain of a terrible ache that came on suddenly. The students don't know what to do. It's rude to fall asleep. Some do know this. Others have never thought about the idea of a house, except for as a box with a triangle on top. If you gave them the concept, they would draw it for you. The students turn their pages to the composition called "Box with Triangle on Top." Look it up in the flat library score shelves. Oh, you can't, because there's no more library. You forgot. Your hair is lighter at the ends because that is the hair that has been with you longest. Louise snips at the ends and lets all the gold drop to the floor. The students sweep it up later with a section of newspaper. In the local section, there is a review of the concert, and news of the fallout.

Out of the Past

is your face fucked into the mattress.

Your body against the tight metal coils.
Your metal lungs up tight against the frame.
Cleopatra with the kohl to black it out.

Yes, though it wrenches,
the picture moves backwards from its spine,
out of the murder. Unspooled from the mystery.
Backed away. Flashed like a sullen stare.

Out of the past is the story of you screwed up
on your hands & knees, all fours, bad dog.
Him owning you like this in the days right before you leave.
You letting him because of leaving him.

And that hole. Mouth full of mattress,
sofa, carpet, base of the spine. It's *common:*
a room, a law, a story you'll tell later and backwards.
A previous life with rage in it, queen of Egypt.
And out the back door.

So, again, out of sequence: up on your damn hands & knees
to greet the love with your gritted teeth.
The hot red thread spilling from your eyes.
The asp in your breast. The fire-ring.
The sick pit like sour cherry just before leave-taking.

In the movie of the now you're the ghost
and narrate *This is also a good position for birthing a child.*

Forest Fire of the ∨

Totally intrinsic, it's got a rural route p.o.,
waits for its ∨ felt missives. It's been known to give bad advices.
Poor thing. It breaks; it aches. It has a mangled
cat-toy of strings that tug and release a familiar melody.
A continual forest fire rages inside it
because a person is having sex then taking cigarettes nearby
and leaving them smoldering in ∨'s satin sheets.
The smoke itself is a factory of plumage,
the curlicues of where two entities divide.
When it can't bear the inconsistencies, a bellied man
with a shotgun is hired to guard the ∨.
In every season, hunters come, drunk on whiskey,
after it. It picks up a hitchhiker to camouflage
its fickle ways, tries to be big about the whole thing,
but it is dry and it always burns. They say ∨ is a burning thing.
Bent on redemption, the ∨ helps a deaf child hang Christmas lights.
The child practically skips for joy, and everything is blurred, blinking halos.
But all the while, ∨ harbors its attack.
The ∨ gets moist and then splits, telling the story
everyone knows, of the redder kiss inside.

Katie Smith Says, "A Woman's Body is a Battleground. I Should Know."

After I was killed they found the perfect nursery, all complete:
soft-backed rocker, the uneasy bones of the changing table draped in lotions,
stacks of flannel squares like milk teeth lined in gum-pink silk.

This is the room to which I would lure her, my full blossom,
my fat thing, so I could cut the baby out to be my valentine.
I called her to pick up some misdelivered things,
gifts we both would need. I took her almost name,
so we could be the twins we were meant to be.

When she came, I faked a deep chorus of rupture,
hurried her in, doubled over.
Like one who knew. I locked the door.
Set at her with my knife-arms.
Clapped my hand to her mouth.
It was to be a kiss.

But biology knows a secret it keeps from the honor roll:
intuition. Self-preservation. Survival.
Adrenaline, that makes the blood go round the clock.
Under my big shirt I had only a toy soldier's heart, melting in tin.
Under hers, the real deal, so she fought back and finished me.

Also, there's the trick of melatonin.
The sun sees better those with babies,
loves them, damages them,
little rivulets of spider blood in their fucking lucky faces.
Breaking them down, thickening their skin. I was and am pale as bird's-eye.
If I kept animals they would have known, too,
and left me be like the soft wolf cast out of the herd.

The dogs all follow the chosen ones, the swollen,
furrow into their pussies, hunting heat and colostrum.

Neighbors, though, are stupid, and believed me.
I had a victory garden registry, all the bounty
of sterile bottles and waterproof sheeting,
tiny silver scissors and nasal bulbs,
plastic nipples to keep the outlets at bay,
desires waiting to be harvested. I will need these things,
I told them all. I need them.

Oh what does it mean to be *warlike*? Like a war?
What does it mean to be *Southern*? *Articulate*?
I lived on God's little acre, in a time of God.
The good people of God. God bless you and goodnight.

My recovered memory pitches again
toward the black-winged fairies like nesting dolls, tiny things flickering
in the thickets of sexual trauma, neglect, burning, holy love.
And do you believe in fairies? Clap your hands if you do.

February 12, 2005

A little ditty I like to call "Stockholm Syndrome"

I kidnap this dog.
She adores me, goes off leash
impeccably, is my own pretty Patty
Hearst. She has lilac-milk eyes and rustproof fur.
She is the cleanest-mouthed friend I've got.
On the way to market, we go over and over our story
in case we're stopped by the cops. When we get to town
we have zany montage adventures with helium
and ping pong balls and when we go on double dates
we pretend to be each other because no one,
not even our best beaus, can tell us apart until the kiss.
And still we're twins. She's my own
Patty Duke, and she comes around the bend in the stairs when I call,
and when she calls I lower my eyes
and never grin, because in her culture
that's the Burt Bacharach Look of Love. I get all of my body down below her
to show her I care. I call her
Mama's Bestest Best Own Sweet Girl and stick by her
in the moonlight in the park, buy her
slices of deli meat I dangle overhead which makes her
thirsty and ill, so then I'm ridden
with guilt and cry for what I've done while she sleeps.
She makes me sorrowful romantic.
She's my own Patsy Cline. She teaches me
tricks and wants discipline. We spend hours
staying right where we are, then go spastic
with the joy of how well we've done at it.
She's Tom Verlaine to my Patti Smith Rimbaud,
and teaches me everything I know.
I know she dreams. She knows that I do.

Her eyes are milk-lilac. Houseless,
we curl up into our double-wide home of two golden bodies,
two golden bodies inside the beautiful wind of a snow globe.

The Fornicators

There were three girls wearing bangles carrying water
and names from the Bible: her cup runs,
her like a cow, her dance whilst her god
lay dying, and each morning that well drew water.

We were them girls. Lightning broke out
of the wood then. When we say it rain
and we worked. Every veil stuck to our whisper.

Lot in life, they said of us, as if salted.
Thieves in the larder what we knew of it.
The blood is someone else's ink, someone who makes writing.
We three, with sapphires. Opal.
Turquoise set deep in the eye.

The blood is someone's ink, someone who makes time go.
We three don't make a mark when the angel comes to tell us
our husband's killed our child and then we die laughing.
What a difference to have fresh-cut flowers.

Two-Lane Blacktop

{We hitchhikt ti th cemtary.
{Me n th Deadr Girl.
{City car what was killt her ma n pa.
{City car what killt m.

This day has some rain in it, where you
Or I could be a black} umbrella.
Either. And graceful or mourning,
It could be our time. Dawn-time,
As passers-through this country. And I could buy
You eggs with the bread we have left.
Or you could panhandle for beer money
This being I think {still} Oklahoma.
Or I myself could be the coming rain sleeping}
With you, only a hunger between us.
I want a piece} of you but I don't
Mean it. I mean I love you. Please honey.
Don't say "not working." Don't say it.
Be morning yellow and I'll give up speed,
Time}, speed. Mouthkiss me in the fog
And we'll break all the minutes into dust}.

{Died on Saturday.
{This a city car.
{City car was thi one what killt m.
{Now thi Girl she don't talk no more.
{She act deadr n dirt.
{We don't drive.
{We take a ride.
{Ten mile on.

Chamberglass

They tell you, *We can't tell you*
what your child will be ever like
and they are telling you the truth.
No one, not you, even knows
if there will be such a child.
It's like an opera in which, slowly,
every person born in the red square
on the bingo card of your birth
is drifting away to death-land,
discarding their white silk scarves and fancy dress
to jumble into a heartland of flat, poor sleeping.
You lie awake in the summer night and think about the truth
how its sound rises with the heat that keeps you waking.

Some have learned to gamble
and you do not love them anymore,
except a little. They were always good at games.
Some are drinking and lying
about it. They cover each number. You have wishes
that are otherwise, an aside
you sing to the audience buried like good friends
in your chamberglass pit,
the body as empty as after the orchestra
has removed its black clothes.

The Turn of the Screw

The biggest influence on me, thanks for asking,
was James: *The Turn of the Screw.* Back in the service kitchen,
I've got a fiancée ruined by it, the tower,
the burning womanly pond, thank god, all her palm-fronds
turn me on, my nudie life drawing model. I got that yearning
from James, a servant you can count on to do her duty,
spurn a child raving in the night and acting slyboots
so she can come to my bed and make headway, oh so bookish.
I got the night from James, but not the dew, and not the sentence—
his churn and churn, a ribbon through some actress'
brilliantly emotive red vagina, the kind that chews the scenery.
My fiancée won't watch the movie as she makes the household stew,
how innocent the young charges act, as if they never swam home,
how the public part of the novella made it plain:
how it influenced me, gave me what to do,
made me its steward, learned me what for, asked me to marry.

The Missing, The Maybe

I.   When they took from me the rotten tooth
        I asked them to take, I asked
        it back, so I could palm and size the hole,
        see the dead grey place on the slick bone.
        So I could keep whole, keep all I own.

        Made from a promise of sand,
        of stars, I wash away with just wind.
        These bones my sail-bones.
        These teeth my anchors.

II.   This is the central text:
        middle of the book with its white silk thread
        cut through like a tooth,
        middle of the page, flocked with red comment.
        These words have been here before.
        History is a spell spelled with dust.

III.   Black witch, white witch.

        Do not let anyone steal away with your hair.
        Anything from your body can be used to make you weak.

        Do not ink the skin that belongs to God, borrower.
        It must return as it came, like clean sheets.
        Perfume the house with sage, the oven
        with salt. Burn your leavened germs to dust.

IV.   Yes, another book about genocide
and my body. And the third element
I cannot recall: tell me again, was it wind?

V.   To make art, I sleep with the face
of another white woman on my face.
To trick the spirits. To redden
their eyes. To keep
my child (I do not have) alive in its rocking bed
I sleep in this glass box like the woman
with the poison apple, waiting without breath. Someone
may make an image of it, but the soul will fly up.
I will curl into my white mask,
an angel in the death-house.

VI.   What of the salted ovens?

VII.   I am meat
(blood, rib lifted from man and sand).
I remember this by keeping an animal at the foot of my bed
like an amulet. We are neither
of us fit for burning. None.

VIII.   Here is the thing about teeth:
        they last a long enamel.

        Sixty years is a mere mother, nothing.

        Germany is a very pretty continent
        I will never see, a grey place in the back of my mouth.

        Poland, Austria.
        I am halfway to sixty, halfway to an attic.

IX.   Before the woman with the poison apple,
        there was a shrieker made from no rib.
        God took her back by the hair.

        White ghost, red ghost.
        They took her bone white child.
        Left her with a gaping mouth.

X.   Now they have excised the smallest bones
        from my feet and I did not remember
        to ask them back so I could keep them. Unwhole,
        I can be screwed to a post,
        possessed, known by my breath to be this yellow star girl.
        I keep an animal with me like an Eden,
        for protection. From God. From history. From the spells.
        Me and her, we speak with the same black tongue.

Hotel

We know. The rooms seem empty.
Our names are in the most lost registers.
We were given a system to cut the life from our mouth.
Or no system. Either way a scream.

All the sheets here are white,
with behind-the-black faces.
You can do a thing with a faucet,
a concussion. This nation knows to bruise.

Death is a very close door in the hall—
see how our foot slips in?
(The sweet taste of shit.)
See how everything, history, is a chute?
See how our tongue, this close door,
is also that black, that sweet?

Fuck us in springtime.
Let the air roll over the mass grave like petals.
It also smells sweet. It is our hair.
It is chalk, bags of rice, nails.
There is a star here called America.
We follow her everywhere.
She is a ball of gas,
a fired-off round, a stove, a blackout.
She keeps us in her kitchen.
We could be anyone.
Under the bed, we are anyone.
Any genocide we've mentioned.

Babel

The Jew who invented Esperanto: he's a Jew,
don't deny it. Not a bone of language
is neutral—it wags like a broken hound,
every inch of scruff from some half-breed.

A Jew tried to bleach his tongue,
make the whole world his pidgin so no one
could tell what he was, but the mama-loshen
suckles with her tainted milk, poison water.
Later he is told *How well you speak,*
how unlike the dirty Jew who invented babble.

The twentieth century is an Esperanto:
it was invented by a Polish Jew
and never worked, the century invented
by Austrian Jews, analysts who peeled
back the brain, nailed back
each gurgling tongue to a door of decrees:
now we speak mongrelese,
and not even half of our words are our own.

The patriarch laughs from his barking throne:
our psyches speak Esperanto,
the towering desperation of the Jew to be clean;
our spirits, the language of a dog.

Museum   *after Robert Wilson*

The milk. The knife. The boy. The water.
The spoon. The hand. The wolf. The glass.
The tongue, eyeless. The house. The bulb.
The dark. The bed. The iron. The needle.
The stone. The half. The cedar. The white.
The collar. The stair. The board. The possible.
The fog. The sink. The milk. The glass.

City of Paper

»I found this piece of paper
with your address on it
so I've mailed it back to you.
I thought you might need some of the numbers.
They seemed private.
I don't know you, but hi.
I found it in my flower box.
I found your name in my ivy.

»I don't believe a thing until I see it written down.
I need it in hard copy.
Do you have something on paper you can send me?

»The city is a city of paper.
We work on it, and when it rains,
paper falls.

»Please fill out this form.
Make sure you complete the reverse.
The yellow copy is yours to keep.

»There has been a flood of paper.
Paper war, paper bomb, paper terror, paper crash.
Paper attack.

»Can you please make a copy for the central file?
Photo-reduce it and save the original.
»The streets are lined with paper.
I have someone else's name now.

»City of ash.

»I don't like reading off a screen—
so impersonal, non-sensual—
so I always print out.
I like to hold something in my hand while I read.

»They spread the paper across the neighborhoods
so everyone could have some.
This is what it can mean to live in a democracy.
The disaster was flesh-bits and twisted steel, as they say,
but even as far away as here we got paper
floating down over us.

»There was a movie about the future
that said "In the future, you will have a lobotomy
and dream you are flying."
The scariest scene in the movie involved paper
flying around in the wind of a future city.
It ruined everything.
It was so out of control.

»We "waded" through paper.
Parted the paper sea to get back home.
»It's funny, because the offices had computers,
you know, but when it rained down
it was paper and not a digital rain.
It's not actually funny.

»The city runs on paper.
We run through the paper city.
In those first moments, we just ran.

»Without the paper records, we can't do business.
It's strange how we still rely on it.
Ancient Egypt and we still haven't replaced it.

»When you think about it, our money is paper
and it can and does burn.
There isn't actually anything to back it up.
It represents invisible gold.

»The lights were out at home, so we went to a coffeeshop.
We ate paper, tasted paper in the soup.

»Great amounts of the city were made into ash
but paper survived.
Some sheets seemed perfectly new, fresh from a ream.
Some had only a word left.

Kafka's *Letter to His Father*

There isn't much you need to know about the story.
It was given to a mother.
The mother gave it back.
The mother came from an odd people.
One sister took over a gypsy farm.
Kafka once stayed at the sister's farm when he was ill.
This sister, and two others, died in the camps or out of them.
The man who lies down with dogs awakens in fleas.
Each page has thirty-four lines.
A long balcony stretched the inner courtyard of Austrian homes.
The letter is long and "has an undertone of despair."
"Sterben" is apparently German for dying.

Governance (A Mystery)

I. In Which I Am a Detective

I am a detective among the gentiles
carrying a magnifier, ink, and my distinct fingerprint
around with me like a stash of weapons.
I leave my bloody hand in the dust of all murders investigated.
No one leaves the room, but since I am alone, I am the prime suspect.

II. In Which I Discover a Hidden Passageway

I know something of bookcases, the backsides
exposed to dungeons of old money. I read the funny papers.
I know every hidden hallway, cut all the latches in my sleep.
I wandered the well-trimmed labyrinth for forty days
and forty nights before I worshipped even one golden charm.
When finally I sinned, there was no dragon.
There were only two rats, me and another.

III. In Which I Practice My Needlework

The other day, I exposed a rat or two in a cloister,
embroidered the charges into a border of scarlet flowers.
It took me the better part of the afternoon and some wormwood.
Then I drowned the evidence like kittens.
Now the ancestral portraits hung in the wide stairs cling to me.
A rodent curls into forelocks inside my soiled prayer vest.

IV. In Which I Make an Oily Miracle

These leather straps they found to bind me?
They are mine, and these goblets. This spice-box.
This little cistern. Mine, mine. I am a kink-haired
Nancy Drew and this is the case of the missing menorah.
Seven brass knuckles on the job and only one flame to guide me.
Still, I complete the war in record time.

V. In Which I Fulfill a Covenant

Four mothers sent me to town with a magic bean
and said *come home with a calf by which we can ruin ourselves.*
I was so happy to comply. I have an oxen cart
fastened at each hip with a wooden stake
and I pull and pull, leaving the good tenths all fallow.
At night I dream of the brothers I've betrayed but they don't bother me.
I am saving my nightmares for the long famine ahead.

VI. In Which I Reveal My Secret Annex

Come closer and let me touch your head.
I will bless you in fever and wish you good luck on occasion.
All of the wayward idolaters—that smallest pupil,
that puppet, that tiny white dog—will be mine.
With a star I will bind them to me and live forever
in this terrible house where I skim the moat for soup.
Hear O Israel the lord is god the lord is one
and I have yet to meet the master of the manor
who hired me and brought me to this strange dead country.

The Tooth Fairy Leaves a Gift for a Tourmaline Mining Disaster

To die by fire takes only a slip of paper,
a tool to make a life from a fortune,
one simple traitor to make a million from a mine.

To burn requires only a back on which to woozy and
sweat that tastes more of crush than meat
so the arson can be fueled by brine.

Two human dogs meet on a rural route.
Both are missing teeth. Both lie.

The engineer says to the hunchback,
"Shoot, I didn't know this marrow was yours!"

It's okay. They're neighbors.
They each live on the other side of the graveyard of pilgrims
that sticks up like molars surrounded by a chain-link fence
for its own protection from time.

The hours have collapsed inwards and died.
No one lives on the *other* other side.
That house is all shuttered up,
its blues and golds and pinks mostly stripped
so that when the arsonist comes
to deliver his holy package of ends,
nothing mutters or brings the flaming gift in from the step.

This town is no place for woodland creatures.
It's the shortest two words in the manual: "we wept."

Exodus 1:6-11

A king went down like the sun behind a hill,
slipping in his golden throne, and a king arose
and the third time a charm: that king
did not know my name.
Did not know our names, how they end
in mountains of stone.

We mean to say he did not know any promise ever made,
or the dream of wheat, or of stars.
A hundred years could have passed
between the first book and these next four
for all he did not know of us.
He was unlike any relation, this new king.

And here we live in the dead city,
winding our favored corpses in dry cloth,
wanting what wants us back
and so do not eat with other wanting.

We reckon with sand. We build the pyramids.
There's a story that goes
in every generation there will be only eleven
who are any good. Another goes
in every generation there will be one who may destroy you.
We suppose the rest stand in corners.

We are getting good at corners.
We miter bricks and have this dull hymn
as our grace:
God are the things we do not control.

One. Two. Three.

YSH LY SHLOSHH DVRYM L'SPR LCH

i have three things to tell you/have to me three things to tell to you(girl)

ACHD: TZYPORH HYE LO SYPR, OH SMCHOT

one: a bird is not a story, or happiness/bird(girl) she no story, or happiness

SHTYM: AYN LI KLOM AMRTY ET H'KL

two: i have nothing. i have said every-thing/not owned to me(genderless) nothingness (in the past)i(gender-less) have said to the all

SHLOSH: H'DVR BTOCH H'SHOLCHN—RK AKSHAV SHMATI ET H'KL

three: the thing in the table—only now have i heard its voice/the thing inside the table—only now i heard(in the past) of the voice.

One. Two. Three.

My father does this thing where he takes away my vowels—it hurts, though there are lozenges, there are guttural movements like small mammals below my words, there is vulnerability: it's such an experiment with no leading cause. He takes away my dots and dashes. Do I still remember the table, its wobbling limbs, my language locked inside? There's a land, a destiny I share with my father while he's in the bath, this floating, cresting genitalia over the table of scientific water, hard science, hard water; and I am progeny, the oldest of three so I have lost my vowels first and am locked in the bathroom while he sings a song. I'm an experiment, it's a psychology, it's about Memory and Cognition, it's about Reading and Retaining, do you see my vowels leaking out and still make my wet sense? My father's father's mother, beloved, began an experiment in which she made the dead words and their vowels, their secret code, rise from the sand to new memory—she did it to children. And thus in a pre-nation, one with new words, a tribe of wet mammals arose, speaking with a new destiny tongue. They named a street for her name, for her voice. This is not a story or a bird you can make sing in the bath, all its consonants splashing; the constant progeny, all her vowels drowned. Out of respect for my grandfather's mother's memory, my father strips away my dashed symbology—it's not modern. In this world, you do not name someone a word unless the original meaning is dead. It is barely an experiment, and too useful. Behold the modernization of an ancient memory: even out of context I hear the voice of this tale on my sill, a missing syllable I can barely reclaim.

Abah sheli ho { } davar kazeh { } { } sheli—{ }, yash { }, yash { } kimo bsarim k'tnim { } h'melim sheli, yash { }; { } kacha { } im af { } { }. Ho kacha et ha { } vi ha { } sheli. Ha'im ani adayin zocheret h'shulchan, ha { } { } shelo, ha lashon sheli { } { }? Yash eretz, { } ani { } im avi kaesher ho { } { }, { } { } { } { } h'shulchan shel mayim { }, { } { }; vani ha bat h'rishonah shel shlosha az ani { } et ha { } sheli h'rishonah vi ani { } { } sharutim { } ho shir shirim. Ani { }, ho psycologia, { } { } { } vi { }, { } { } { } vi { }, haim atem roim et ha { } sheli { } vi adiyin { } { } { }? Ema shel aba shel avi, chaviva, { } { } { } he osa ha milim ha { } vi { }, { } { }, olim mayha { } li { } chadash—he asah et zeh l'yiladim. Vi az bi eretz { }, eretz im milim chadashim, { } { } { } alo, midabrim im lashon { } chadash. Haym karu et derech ba sham shelah, li kol shelah. Zeh lo sipur o tziporah sheh atem { } shir bi { }, kol h'{ } { }; { } { }, kol ha { } { }. Mey { } bishviel hazikaron li emah she safti, avi { } { } { } sheli—zeh lo { }. B'olam hazeh, atem lo korim li'mishehu { } ha { } ha { } b'mavet. Zeh { } { } { }, vi yotar m'dai { }. Henah ha { } shel zikaron { }: { } { } { } ani shoma'h h'kol shel ha'sipur hazeh al { } sheli, { } { } { } { } { }.

What I remember is only what belongs to me.

Gospel

No stab in these hands.
No thorns. No myrrh.

No swing low.
No jubilee.
No abide with me,
not in this hymnal.

But blow me open, God.
No song in this throat,
just blow me open.

Synopsis

I will martyr myself at the stake, singing *Hear*.
A snake knew my name and caressed me.
The bush burned with ideas.
I was speechless; I was a ruby.
Every generation fashions an enemy.
I hid under a trapdoor in Spain, crying half-language.
Coveting, coveting, yes, no, like a jezebel on a rooftop terrace.
I eat nothing containing cartilage.
The oven is full of rock salt.
I went with my brother to interpret his stammering.
The first-born son must fast all morning.
I entered a beauty contest of strangers.
The rains lasted forever, like white dresses.
A dove came by with a postcard.
I killed my brother and hid.
There were dreams of stars and wheat.
The graves are decorated with only stones.
I took a literal train to my death. It was on time.
Boys are plied with wine and snipped.
I pray according to daylight.
Next year will return to the city of gold.
I shield my eyes from the priests' blessing.
Girls get two candles each.
I stood at the bottom of a mountain with my soul.
A very small parcel of real estate was promised.
I was taken for a fool by my village to make a story.
He offered the angels his most finely sifted flour.
I hid in an attic with my diary.
The tents are goodly.
I was a lost tribe and came out black.

Each breastplate held a dozen precious gems.

The sea boiled and horses drowned.

I hope not to be inscribed in the book of the damned.

A drop of oil burned for eight days.

I win money made of bitter chocolate.

The cat swallows the chicken, and the reaper swift behind.

I made love to my king like a sibling in a cave.

Three, four, eight, eighteen, forty, one hundred and twenty.

Trees are planted like children there.

I pretended to be my younger sister under the veil.

Manna rained down and tasted like muffins.

I looked back and was turned to salt.

Rams, bulls, lambs and billy goats.

I offered you something clean from a well.

A prophet slips in the door to drink from his cup.

I hid from God and was found.

ACKNOWLEDGMENTS

The Kafka epigraph is from *The Basic Kafka*, with an introduction by Erich Heller (Washington Square Press/Pocket Books, 1979). The Celan epigraph to "Pastoral" is from John Felstiner's translation.

Many thanks to the editors of the journals in which these poems first appeared: *American Letters & Commentary:* "The Turn of the Screw"; *American Poetry Review:* "Chamberglass," "Me and Peter Lorre Down by the Schoolyard"; *Barrow Street:* "Morning Breaks the Window," "Home Décor"; *Black Clock:* "Private, I"; *Black Warrior Review:* "Please Be Good," "At the Cinema Lecture"; *Bridge:* "Report," "Letters from Camp"; *Caffeine Destiny:* "Some Dark Holler"; *The Canary:* "Saints"; *Columbia Poetry Review:* "Little Red Fox"; *Conjunctions:* "Purple Noon," "Two-Lane Blacktop," "Stag Movie," "Center Field"; *Denver Quarterly:* "The First American to Walk on the Moon Was Black," "What Would You Do Without Houses?"; *Gulf Coast:* "Shirley Temple, Black"; *First Intensity:* "Kafka Bicentennial"; *jubilat:* "The Tooth Fairy Leaves a Gift for a Tourmaline Mining Disaster"; *Octopus:* "Heenayni"; *Parakeet:* "Museum"; *Pleiades:* "City of Paper," "Cannibal Flotation Device"; *Rhino:* "Pentecost"; *Sentence:* "Pastoral"; *6x6:* "Folding the Bed"; *3rd Bed:* "Analogies"; *UR-VOX:* "Proverbs 31:10-31"; *Verse:* "Secret Lesbian Tee-Off."

"Honey" first appeared on The American Academy of Poets website; thanks to the Academy.

Heartfelt gratitude to the MacDowell Colony, where many of these poems were written, and to the friends I made there; my residency had an enormous impact. Thanks to my colleagues and students in the English Department at Columbia College Chicago (especially David Trinidad for his comments on this manuscript) and to my family and friends (especially those who helped me with this book—D'vora, Rachel, Michael Burkard, Tobin Anderson, Suzanne Buffam and Chicu Reddy). Thanks also to Joyelle McSweeney and Johannes Göransson, who made this the book I hoped it could be and gave it such a good home. Finally, this book would not have been written were it not for my beloved family: Rob Morris, our daughter Willa, and the real little red fox, our dog Maisie.

My deep thanks also to Lyn Hejinian and David Lehman for selecting "Saints" for *Best American Poetry 2004* and to Paul Muldoon and David Lehman for selecting *"The Turn of the Screw"* for *Best American Poetry 2005*.

ABOUT THE AUTHOR

Arielle Greenberg is the author of *Given* (Verse 2002) and the chapbook *Fa(r)ther Down: Songs from the Allergy Trials* (New Michigan, 2003). She is co-editing, with Rachel Zucker, an anthology of essays on women poets and mentorship forthcoming from Wesleyan University Press. She teaches in the graduate and undergraduate poetry programs at Columbia College Chicago and lives in Evanston, IL, with her family.

ACTION BOOKS TITLES 2005

Remainland: Selected Poems of Aase Berg
Scandinavian Series #1
Johannes Göransson, Translator
ISBN 0-9765692-0-5

The Hounds of No by Lara Glenum
ISBN 0-97656592-1-3

My Kafka Century by Arielle Greenberg
ISBN 0-9765692-2-1

www.actionbooks.org